THE LITTLE GUIDE TO

FORMULA ONE

Published in 2024 by OH!
An Imprint of Welbeck Non-Fiction Limited,
part of Welbeck Publishing Group.
Offices in: London – 20 Mortimer Street, London W1T 3JW
and Sydney – level 17, 207 Kent St, Sydney NSW 2000 Australia
www.welbeckpublishing.com

Compilation text © Welbeck Non-Fiction Limited 2023
Design © Welbeck Non-Fiction Limited 2023

Disclaimer:
This publication may contain copyrighted material, the use of which has not
been specifically authorised by the copyright owner. The material in this
publication is made available in this book under the fair use and intended only
for review, research and news reporting purposes only. The publisher is not
associated with any names, teams or associations. All trademarks, copyright,
quotations, company names, registered names, products, characters,
logos and catchphrases used or cited in this book are the property of their
respective owners. This book is a publication of OH! An imprint of Welbeck
Publishing Group Limited and has not been licensed, approved, sponsored,
or endorsed by any person or entity.

All rights reserved. No part of this publication may be reproduced, stored
in a retrieval system, or transmitted in any form or by any means (including
electronic, mechanical, photocopying, recording, or otherwise) without prior
written permission from the publisher.

ISBN 978-1-80069-620-4

Compiled and written by: David Clayton
Editorial: Victoria Denne
Project manager: Russell Porter
Production: Arlene Lestrade

A CIP catalogue record for this book is available from the British Library

Printed in China

10 9 8 7 6 5 4 3 2 1

THE LITTLE GUIDE TO

FORMULA ONE

HIGH-OCTANE QUOTES
FROM THE PITS TO THE PODIUM

CONTENTS

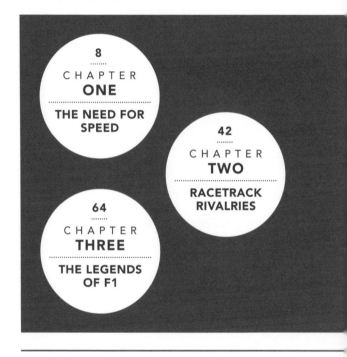

INTRODUCTION

The Little Book of Formula One includes quotes from some of the greatest racing drivers of all time, including Ayrton Senna, Lewis Hamilton, Max Verstappen, Alain Prost, Nigel Mansell, Niki Lauda, Stirling Moss, and many, many more.

What makes these men risk life and limb to hurtle around a track at breakneck speeds? And what are the personalities of those behind the wheel really like?

There are drivers who are deep thinkers, there are drivers with a lust for danger and there are the loveable rogues who bring additional colour and controversy to the most thrilling motorsport competition on the planet.

The Little Book of Formula One is full of insight, knowledge and, at times, deadpan humour that will make you smile, laugh out loud and everything in-between.

From the cutting wit of Kimi Räikkönen to the playful teasing of James Hunt, there are endless nuggets of wisdom and off-the-cuff reactions from the best F1 drivers that have walked the planet. Plus, there's a selection of the commentators' often hilarious observations - step forward, Murray Walker (among others)!

Also included in the pages that follow are facts and trivia about the sport that has captivated billions around the globe for more than seven decades.

CHAPTER
ONE

The Need for Speed

Why F1 racing drivers do
what they do – their passion,
compulsion and determination
to race and be the best...

"

The smell of fuel, driving on the limit on the edge of sliding, it just gives you a lot of adrenaline.

"

Max Verstappen

F1's youngest ever race winner reflects on why he loves doing what he does (2017)

"

If everything is under control you are just not driving fast enough.

"

Stirling Moss

British racing star Moss on the need to push the envelope...

❝

Life would be very boring
without feelings, without
emotions. And there are some
feelings that only we [Formula
One drivers] can experience.
It's a fortunate and unique
position to be in, but it's stressful
at the same time.

❞

Ayrton Senna

Quote from the 2004 book The Life of Senna

66

I feel like people
are expecting me to fail;
therefore, I expect
myself to win.

99

Lewis Hamilton

*Multi-time World Champion Hamilton tells Serena
Williams how he turns negatives into positives in
Interview Magazine (July 2017)*

F1 facts

An F1 car can
accelerate
from 0 to 60 mph
(100 km/h) in
2.6 seconds and
0 to 100 mph
(160 km/h) in
4.0 seconds!

That's fast...

"

I've always believed that you should never, ever give up and you should always keep fighting even when there's only a slightest chance.

"

Michael Schumacher

The German F1 legend's prophetic words from 2007

"

Either winning, or breaking a record, losing, going through a corner at a speed that a few seconds before you didn't think you could, failing, feeling luck, feeling anger, enthusiasm, stress or pain. Only we can experience the feeling and level of it.

"

Ayrton Senna

Another quote from The Life of Senna (2004), as Ayrton describes the uniqueness of the F1 driver…

66

Remember, we win and lose together. I will keep pushing for you guys.

99

Lewis Hamilton

Hamilton on the importance of the team behind him – from the guys in the pit lanes, to the technicians, family members and fans (2014)

66

When you give up your hunger for success you are not racing full-heartedly anymore. Just to be there, that is not my style.

99

Felipe Massa

The Brazilian driver laments his one-point loss to Lewis Hamilton in the 2008 Drivers' Championship by vowing to bounce back...

"

Nothing can really prepare you for when you get in the Formula One car. Knowing that you're driving a multimillion-dollar car, and if you crash it it's going to cost a lot of money, and they might not give you another chance, is scary.

"

Lewis Hamilton

❝

Nobody else can, considering that in our profession we deal with ego a lot, with danger, with our health, continuously, second after second, not just day after day or month after month or year after year. Our life goes by in seconds or milliseconds.

❞

Ayrton Senna

*Insightful quote by the Brazilian from the 2004 book
The Life of Senna*

66

Winning is one thing,
but out of losing I always
learned more. Because
you don't waste time
blaming somebody else.
Analyse yourself. Change
yourself to be successful.

99

Niki Lauda

*Austrian three-time World Champion Niki Lauda's
typically thought-provoking words that have
inspired millions*

"

Racing, competing, it's
in my blood. It's part
of me, it's part of my life;
I have been doing it all
my life and it stands out
above everything else.

"

Ayrton Senna

"

It's hard to drive at the limit, but it's harder to know where the limits are.

"

Stirling Moss

British F1 legend Moss attempts to reveal the complexity of the unknown...

"

The danger sensation is exciting. The challenge is to find new dangers.

"

Ayrton Senna

The Brazilian reveals the endless lust F1 drivers have to push the boundaries

"

I was 14 and watching the
Monaco Grand Prix on TV with
my dad. He said, 'That's where
the Formula One drivers live.'
I set my heart on it then – and
I made my formula one debut
in 1994 and moved to Monaco
in 1995.

"

David Coulthard

The British driver – winner of 13 Grand Prix races –
reveals how he followed his dream and moved to one of
F1's most iconic destinations (2004)

"

I always knew about the risks I was taking. Every year, someone you knew was killed racing. You had to ask yourself, do you enjoy driving these cars so much that you're prepared to take that risk?

"

Niki Lauda

Lauda reflects in The Official Ferrari Magazine *how tragedies made him re-think his racing career (2012)*

66

That's what I enjoy –
always driving on the limit
of what you can do.

99

Max Verstappen

*A maxim that would serve the World Champion well in
the years ahead... (2017)*

66

People don't understand
that it was maybe my
biggest pleasure to drive
an F1 car when it's wet.

99

Alain Prost

*French driver Prost reveals his love of driving in the
driving rain! (1993)*

66

Qualifying is all about putting everything that you have, and that the car has in one lap. It's like a rush, I really enjoy that.

99

Sebastian Vettel

Four-time German World Champion on his love for that one, magical lap that can pre-determine a race (2011)

"

In life, it's winning – when
I go to the supermarket,
and I go with a friend,
I try to get through the
door first. Things like that
– everything in life is a
competition for me.

"

Fernando Alonso

*Spanish driver Alonso explains why you shouldn't
go shopping with him...*

Interviewer: "How does it feel to drive at 300 km/h?"

Kimi: "It feels normal."

2007 F1 World Champion Kimi Räikkönen
reveals that driving fast comes naturally... to some!

"

I was a driver and a racer.
The difference between drivers,
who can be great World
Champions, and racers, who
are also World Champions, is
that racers don't wait for
things to happen: they make
things happen.

"

Nigel Mansell

*Mansell reflects on a career that saw him crowned
F1 champion in 1992 (2014)*

66

In my sport, the quick
are too often listed among
the dead.

99

Jackie Stewart

*Three-time World Champion Jackie Stewart on the
perils of the sport's risk-takers...*

"

If you don't come walking back to the pits every once in a while holding a steering wheel in your hands, you're not trying hard enough.

"

Mario Andretti

US F1 driver Andretti – winner of one World Championship – on how chasing victory can sometimes end up with an early walk back to the pits... (1978)

> ## "
> I've tried everything other than jumping out of a plane, but nothing gives you an adrenaline rush like racing a car.
> ## "

Nigel Mansell

The former F1 World Champion reflects on a life less ordinary in an interview with The Times (2006)

"

Jolly hard work.

"

James Hunt

Responding to the question:
"What's it like to drive in a Grand Prix?" on the
children's TV show Magpie (1975)

"

It's correct that I'm a bad loser. Why should I lie? If I was good at losing I wouldn't be in Formula One. I think it's more honest to act how you really feel than pretending to be the smiling boy who actually isn't in the mood to smile.

"

Sebastian Vettel

Honesty was always the best policy for the German driver...

"

A lot of people criticize Formula One as an unnecessary risk. But what would life be like if we only did what is necessary?

"

Niki Lauda

Austrian Lauda succinctly nails the essence of Formula One, as he so often did

"

Does it scare me,
driving into nothing at
300kph?
Of course it does – I'm
not an idiot.

"

Alain Prost

Ask a stupid question...

"

It is amazing how many drivers, even at the Formula One level, think that the brakes are for slowing the car down.

"

Mario Andretti

One that the American speedster may need to explain to the average driver!

"

To achieve anything in this game, you must be prepared to dabble in the boundary of disaster.

"

Stirling Moss

British racing legend, who was partially paralysed for six months after a serious accident, on the dangers each F1 driver with burning ambition faces every time they race (1962)

CHAPTER
TWO

Racetrack Rivalries

The duels, dislike and sometimes grudging respect of the drivers who crossed swords on and off the racetrack – and occasionally even praised their nemesis.

"

Ayrton has a small problem: he thinks he can't kill himself, because he believes in God, and I think it is pretty dangerous for other drivers.

"

Alain Prost

"

Because I believe in God and have faith in God, it doesn't mean I'm immortal, it doesn't mean I'm immune, as has been claimed. I am as scared as anyone of getting hurt, especially driving a Formula One car. It's a constant danger.

"

Ayrton Senna

"

Alain Prost has taken the
advantage, Senna is trying to go
through on the inside...
[collision occurs] and it's happened
immediately! This is amazing!
Senna goes off at the first corner,
but what has happened to Prost?
He has gone off too!
Well, that is amazing, but I fear,
absolutely predictable.

"

Murray Walker

*Legendary F1 commentator Murray Walker describes
the controversial collision between Prost and his nemesis
Senna at the 1990 Japanese Grand Prix*

66

Sometimes I admit
I was frightened by him;
he was prepared to
do anything.

99

Alain Prost

*Recalling his first physical altercation with
Ayrton Senna after they became team mates at
McLaren in 1988 as Senna aggressively
shoved Prost towards the pit wall at Estoril.
As seen on Motorsport.com (May 2018)*

"

Mansell is argumentative, he's rude and he's got a really ugly wife.

"

Nelson Picquet

The Brazilian driver's feud with Williams team-mate Nigel Mansell oversteps the mark somewhat in a 1988 Playboy magazine interview

"

He's arrogant, and after
he started winning
races he started treating
everyone really badly.
Besides which, he's
written off piles of cars.
No one wanted him
to win.

"

Nelson Picquet

More Picquet vitriol aimed at British driver
Nigel Mansell (1988)

"

When I was teammates with Piquet and Prost, they were prolific in what they would get up to undermine you.

"

Nigel Mansell

Mansell's very British response to the antics of former Williams duo – and occasional mischief makers – Alain Prost and Nelson Picquet (2014)

“

But when you're a World Champion, or multi-World Champion, and then you're beating them in a number two car like I was with Nelson Piquet with Williams, he wasn't my best friend was he?!

”

Nigel Mansell

Mansell reflects on his rivalry with Nelson Picquet – ever so slightly rubbing salt in! (2014)

66

Alain will do everything
in his power to win,
he doesn't like getting
beaten by anyone
and least of all me.

99

Nigel Mansell

> 66

Mika Häkkinen was the best
opponent [I've had] in terms
of his quality, but the biggest
admiration I had for him was
we had 100% fight on track but a
totally disciplined life off track.
We respected each other highly
and let each other live quietly.

99

Michael Schumacher

*Seven-time World Champion Schumacher reflecting on
the driver he admired more than any other...*

"

I remember, before I got to
Formula One, being a huge fan
of Kimi's and when I played the
computer games, I'd always
be in Kimi's car, so this crazy
experience of racing against
him, losing a championship to
him and then seeing lots of great
battles, and so he will be missed.

"

Lewis Hamilton

*Lewis Hamilton after Kimi Räikkönen's
2021 retirement...*

"

If there's a red light when
you leave the pitlane
you have to stop. Then
some wooden eye [Lewis
Hamilton] crashes into
you and breaks the car.

"

Kimi Räikkönen

*Finnish star Räikkönen is unimpressed after being
rear-ended in the pit lane by the young British driver
at the 2008 Canadian Grand Prix*

66

Ayrton and I shared a lot of incredible races, where he was first, and I was second and vice versa. I think it's fair to say I am the only racer in Grand Prix history who wasn't intimidated by him, and I think that was great for the fans – it did make us have a few close calls, though!

99

Nigel Mansell

Mansell recalls his rivalry with Ayrton Senna in an interview with Motorsport magazine (2009)

"

I feel really sorry for Niki, I feel sorry for everybody that the race had to be run in such ridiculous circumstances, and quite honestly, you know I wanted to win the championship, and I felt that I deserved to win the championship. I also felt that Niki deserved to win the championship, and I just wish we could have shared it.

"

James Hunt

James Hunt claims his first World Drivers' Championship with a third-place finish, enough to pip Niki Lauda who withdrew from the race believing it should have been cancelled due to torrential rain (1976)

"

I went to the airport.
I told this Japanese taxi driver
to listen to the radio and tell me
who had won the title.
And exactly when the end of the
race came on the radio he drove
through the tunnel of the airport
and the radio stopped.
And when we came out, it was
over. Who won? I asked. 'I don't
know,' he said...

But then, as we came up the ramp to the airport, there was a Ferrari man who wanted to say goodbye. And I looked at his face and I knew straight away. 'Fuck,' I thought. And he said, yes, Hunt was World Champion. So I went home.

"

Niki Lauda

Niki famously chose not to drive in the Japanese Grand Prix due to the treacherous racing conditions – and saw Hunt crowned champion in his absence (1976)

F1 facts

Some F1 teams
consist of more than
600 working members –
one of the reasons
drivers celebrate with
each and every trackside
member of the team
after a successful race.

"

Even now, all these years later,
it's difficult for me to talk about
Ayrton, and not only because
he's not here anymore.
When he died, I said I felt a part
of me had died also, because
our careers had been so bound
together. I know some people
thought I wasn't sincere, but
I meant it.

"

Alain Prost

Alain Prost reflects on the death of his greatest rival
Ayrton Senna (2014)

66

What do you want me to say?! I haven't spoken to him. He's having a smoke and a pancake.

99

Lewis Hamilton

Lewis Hamilton channels his inner 'Goldmember' character from Austin Powers when asked how he felt about Max Verstappen's eighth straight race win at the Belgian Grand Prix – just one short of Sebastian Vettel's record of nine consecutive victories (2023)

"

We will miss him because obviously he has been [in F1] for many years and we had great battles. In the past, more because we had more competitive cars and we were fighting for championships and podiums and things like that.

"

Fernando Alonso

Spaniard Alonso - Räikkönen's championship rival and teammate at Ferrari in 2014 - looks back on a feisty but enjoyable past with the Finn (2021)

CHAPTER
THREE

The Legends of F1

The drivers who have etched
their name into F1 immortality
and their words of wisdom...

66

Every year we find
something new,
we go faster, and that's
what Formula One
is about.

99

Michael Schumacher

"

I put everything in that last lap, it was very emotional when I crossed the line. It was all I had, I gave it all.

"

Sebastian Vettel

The German driver on surpassing Nigel Mansell's 19-year record for most pole positions by securing a 15th of the season in São Paulo (2011)

"

I always thought records were there to be broken...

"

Michael Schumacher

And he broke many...

66

I continuously go further
and further learning
about my own limitations,
my body limitation,
psychological limitations.
It's a way of life for me.

99

Ayrton Senna

*The much-missed Brazilian star on his constant
quest for self-discovery…*

"

The main thing is to be yourself
and not allow people to disturb
you and change you. You have to
be yourself, even though many
times you make a mistake due to
your own personality. You learn,
and you must learn through
your mistakes and get better.

"

Ayrton Senna

66

Formula One drivers were like
gods to me, growing up.

99

Jenson Button

*The British former World Champion reflects
on his inspirations in his book*
Life to the Limit: My Autobiography (2017)

66

The fans always embraced me
because of my driving style, even
when I was on the back foot, if I
didn't have the best car, engine,
or was number two in the team,
I still gave it my all. It didn't
matter where I was on the grid,
I would drive the backside of the
car. Fans loved that I think.

99

Nigel Mansell

*Mansell reflects on the attributes that made him a 'man
of the people' during his F1 career (2014)*

66

Aerodynamics are for people who can't build engines.

99

Enzo Ferrari

Former F1 star Enzo Ferrari scoffs at constructers who tried different means to get their cars to go faster (1960)

66

I am an artist. The track is my canvas, and my car is my brush.

99

Graham Hill

One of F1's most famous quotes... from Britain's two-time World Champion Graham Hill...

"
Formula 1 would be
a paradise without the
media.

"

Kimi Raikkonen

*The Finn's famous disdain for the world's press was
never far from the surface!*

"

In racing there are always things you can learn, every single day. There is always space for improvement, and I think that applies to everything in life.

"

Lewis Hamilton

Wise words from a World Champion with a wise head on his shoulders...

"

Everyone loves a winner.
That's just how the world
is. And Ayrton Senna
was one of the greatest
winners this sport has
ever had...

"

Lewis Hamilton

66

You either commit
yourself as a professional
racing driver that's
designed to win races or
you come second or you
come third or fifth and
I am not designed to
come third, fourth or fifth.
I race to win.

99

Ayrton Senna

The Brazilian's winning mentality was always evident...

> When Michael Schumacher came on the scene, he tweaked the drivers of his time because that's what exceptional drivers do, you break onto the scene and don't simply move out of the way of the legends.

David Coulthard

66

I've accomplished more than I ever dreamed. But I'm hungry for more.

99

Lewis Hamilton

True champions always want more... as quoted in Men's Health (2017)

"

To do something well is so
worthwhile that to die trying to
do it better cannot be foolhardy.
It would be a waste of life to do
nothing with one's ability, for
I feel that life is measured in
achievement, not in years alone.

"

Bruce McLaren

*New Zealand F1 driver Bruce McLaren – whose name
lives on with the McLaren Racing Team today – wrote
this poignant observation after the tragic death of
team-mate Timmy Mayer in Australia (1965)*

"

Patience is a virtue in life, of course, but it's not something we F1 people have too much of.

"

Niki Lauda

The Austrian Formula One champion on the lack of one particular virtue in Grand Prix racers

"

I hate losing.
It doesn't matter if it's
racing or playing ping
pong – I hate it.

"

Lewis Hamilton

*Bad loser Lewis – as quoted in Interview Magazine
(July 2017)*

66

With regard to
performance, commitment,
effort, dedication, there is
no middle ground.
Or you do something very
well or not at all.

99

Ayrton Senna

"

Excuse me, I'm fit,
I don't care a f**k about
the championship.
I want to get back to work.
Simple.

"

Niki Lauda

*Just six weeks after his horrific 1976 accident at
Nürburgring, Niki Lauda decided the only way to move
forward was to race again... as quoted in Ferrari Official
Magazine (May 2019)*

"

On a given day, a given circumstance, you think you have a limit. And you then go for this limit, and you touch this limit, and you think, 'Okay, this is the limit'. And so you touch this limit, something happens, and you suddenly can go a little bit further.

"

Ayrton Senna

More inspirational words from the late, great Brazilian...

66

I am not a driver,
I am a racer.

99

Stirling Moss

Who would argue with such a Formula One great?

"

I'd rather be probably out of second and third place, so I don't have to go to the prize-giving.

"

Kimi Räikkönen

The colourful Finn – lover of only one place on the podium

> **“**
> I have no idols.
> I admire
> work, dedication,
> and competence.
> **”**

Ayrton Senna

"

When I drove for British teams... they called me The Tadpole because I was too small to be a frog.

"

Alain Prost

Frenchman Prost on the subject of Francophobia during his time with McLaren (1994)

66

It shows how much you can touch people, and as much as you can try to give those people, somehow it is nothing compared to what they live in their own mind, in their dreams, for you.

99

Ayrton Senna

"

There are two things no man will admit he cannot do well: drive and make love.

"

Stirling Moss

Moss speaking with more than a grain of truth!

"

Overtaking is one thing. That is an art. But defending as well. You should be able to defend your position.

"

Max Verstappen

The Dutch master – as quoted on BBC Sport (2017)

66

Everything that I've gotten out of life was obtained through dedication and a tremendous desire to achieve my goals... a great desire for victory, meaning victory in life, not as a driver.

99

Ayrton Senna

> **"**
> Do you know why I really love my helmet that much? Because it makes me 15 centimetres taller!
> **"**

Alain Prost

Typical humour from the pint-sized French champion!

66

The sport would not survive today if drivers were being killed at the rate they were in the 1960s and '70s. It would have been taken off the air.
It is beamed into people's living rooms on Sunday afternoons, with children watching.

99

Damon Hill

British driver Damon Hill – the 1996 F1 World Champion – on the safety improvements that kept F1 a family watch...

66

When I notice a rear wheel overtaking me, I know I'm sitting in a Lotus.

99

Graham Hill

A damning verdict by Graham Hill on the Lotus F1 car. This quote was because of a crash Hill was involved in while driving a Lotus that ended with him suffering two broken legs at the 1969 Spanish Grand Prix

“

Just tell her that I won't be dancing for two weeks.

”

Graham Hill

Hill's typically British response to breaking both legs was to ask for the above message to be sent to his wife! (1969)

66

You win a race, the next race it's a question mark. Are you still the best or not? That's what is funny. But that's what is interesting. And that's what is challenging. You have to prove yourself every time.

99

Michael Schumacher

"

I always try to get the best result out of it, I'm not there to just sit second or sit third. I'm a winner, and I want to win every single race, and I will always go for it.

"

Max Verstappen

The Dutch F1 ace defends his swashbuckling race style after his aggressive manoeuvres attract criticism – as quoted on GPFans.com (March 2019)

> **"** That is an important part of my success. Another big part of my success is that I hated not to finish a race. **"**

Alain Prost

"The Professor" discusses his racing strategy (1993)

> ❝
>
> # My biggest error? Something that is to happen yet.
>
> ❞

Ayrton Senna

A sadly prophetic question and answer for the brilliant F1 star who would be tragically killed at the 1994 San Marino Grand Prix as he claims pole position at Monza (1990)

"

With driving a motor car, the danger is a very necessary ingredient. Like if you're cooking, you need salt. You can cook without salt, but it doesn't have the flavour.

"

Stirling Moss

Life in the middle lane was never for Stirling...
(circa 1961)

"

Whoever you are, no matter
what social position you have,
rich or poor, always show great
strength and determination
and always do everything with
much love and deep faith
in God. One day you will reach
your goal.

"

Ayrton Senna

Inspirational words from an inspirational man...

❝

When you walk the track and you see a corner and realise you were going round it at 160mph, you wonder who could be so stupid to take a corner at that speed? But in the car, you don't even think about that.

❞

Sebastian Vettel

Former World Champion Vettel questions F1 drivers and their sanity! As quoted in the Telegraph (2011)

CHAPTER
FOUR

The Mavericks and Enigmas

Individuals who added panache,
derring-do and magic dust to
Formula One racing...

"

There's a lie that all drivers tell themselves. Death is something that happens to other people, and that's how you find the courage to get in the car in the first place. The closer you are to death the more alive you feel. But more powerful than fear itself, is the will to win.

"

James Hunt

"Hunt the Shunt" lifts the lid on what really drives Grand Prix racers... (circa 1976)

66

There are only three sports: bullfighting, motor racing, and mountaineering; all the rest are merely games.

99

Ernest Hemingway

Author, adventurer, enigma... Ernest Hemingway would have made a fine Grand Prix driver

"

Sometimes you've just got to lick the stamp and send it.

"

Daniel Ricciardo

Aussie maverick Ricciardo responds to the question about his daredevil overtaking at the 2018 Chinese Grand Prix

"

Nine points, 20,000 dollars and a lot of happiness. And can I grab that cigarette off you?

"

James Hunt

After what would be his only British Grand Prix victory at Silverstone, Hunt was asked what the win meant to him – before asking a bystander for a few puffs on their cigarette... (1977)

"

The racing driver's
mind has to have the
ability to have amazing
anticipation, coordination,
and reflex. Because of the
speed the car goes.

"

Emerson Fittipaldi

"

I do not speak the English so good, but then I speak the driving very well.

"

Emerson Fittipaldi

Two-time World Champion Fittipaldi spoke the language of Formula One perfectly...

Martin Brundle: "Kimi, you missed the presentation by Pelé."

Kimi: "Yeah."

Martin: "Will you get over it?"

Kimi: "Yeah. I was having a shit."

Raikkonen stole the show at the 2006 Brazilian Grand Prix after missing a presentation from football legend Pelé to Michael Schumacher – with the German driver retiring from the sport for the first time

"

Sex: breakfast of champions.

"

James Hunt

*Perhaps James Hunt's most famous quote –
and one that summed up his personality and
lifestyle perfectly...*

"

It's kids, isn't it? Kids with not enough experience, doing a good job and then they f**k it all up.

"

Mark Webber

Sebastian Vettel, driving for Toro Rosso in his debut season, is chided after crashing into the back of Webber during the safety car period at the 2007 Japanese Grand Prix. This would also cost the Australian his first win in F1...

66

All you need to know about racing you can learn from Super Mario Kart.

99

Jenson Button

British driver Button shares F1's best-kept secret in his book Life to the Limit: My Autobiography (2017)

66

Don't go to men who are
willing to kill themselves
driving in circles looking
for normality.

99

James Hunt

66

I was just having a
shower, and thinking
'Mate, you're lucky to be
in one piece'.

99

Mark Webber

*Aussie F1 star Webber reflects on his good fortune
after a 190mph crash at the 2010 European Grand Prix
during which he spectacularly somersaulted
through the air*

❝

Seatbelts were not yet
compulsory and I didn't
have them because
I couldn't afford them.
Had I been wearing one,
I might have drowned.

❞

James Hunt

*Hunt recalls a time he ditched into water and was
submerged – but was thankfully able to escape without
the issue of freeing himself from a seatbelt first...*

"

What Räikkönen did is
like a breath of fresh air.
We have to understand
that a young driver is not
a robot. As long as he is
not drinking the night
before a race, why not?

"

Flavio Briatore

*Renault boss Briatore backs Kimi Räikkönen's off-track
antics at a London lap-dancing club (2006)*

❝

The problem is, when you're in
the public, people expect you to
perform. You're treated a bit like
an animal in the zoo. They come
up to you and prod you and poke
you to see how you will react.

❞

James Hunt

*James on what life was like as a Formula One
champion - as quoted in Thames TV's Drive In (1977)*

"

The sound of that V10,
a rich growl that reached
right into my soul.

"

Jenson Button

*Button describes what drew him to Formula One in the
first place... as quoted in his book Life to the Limit: My
Autobiography (2017)*

F1 facts

The most successful
constructors team
in F1 is Ferrari, with
16 championships
– however,
Ferrari's last success
was in 2008.

66

NASCAR is a bunch of farmers driving around in circles.

99

Eddie Irvine

*British driver Irvine shares his disdain for NASCAR
and the skills needed to compete...*

66

To hell with safety.
All I want to do is race.

99

James Hunt

66

My life would be much more easier had I been a F1 driver in the '70s with the guys. I was definitely born in the wrong era.

99

Kimi Räikkönen

The controversial Finn admits he would have been a better fit in a different era...

"

I'm not interested in what people think about me. I'm not Michael Schumacher.

"

Kimi Räikkönen

The feisty Finn – a law unto himself...

"

If I get into a car on a
circuit, I drive as fast as
I can; that's it!

"

James Hunt

*The irrepressible Hunt describes his role
as a Formula One competitor as simply as he can...*

"

I'm going to retire, mate. A lot of vomiting going on... I am going to try and stay out. A lot of vomit in the car.

"

Mark Webber

Webber battled the effects of food poisoning during the 2007 Japanese Grand Prix and was on course to challenge for victory until he was forced off the track by Sebastian Vettel...

> ## 66
> # If I wasn't me,
> # I'd want to be me.
> ## 99

Eddie Irvine

The British driver was clearly happy with his lot!

> 66
>
> The drivers in our teams have been and are World Champions, and yet the title is being fought between one driver who is a semi-pensioner and another who is a decent bloke but is like a roadside post.
>
> 99

Flavio Briatore

The former Renault boss's take on the 2009 championship battle between Jenson Button and Rubens Barrichello – hardly flattering for either driver!

F1 facts

A Formula One race car has more than 80,000 assembled parts and takes up 150,000 man-hours to put together from the first piece to the last.

"

I read somewhere that I drive with the luck of a drunk.

"

Kimi Räikkönen

"

When I take go-karts out
with my friends, it's a
disaster normally. But in the
race car, I'm calm because
they pay me to do this, and
I have to be professional.

"

Fernando Alonso

Why the safest place for the Spaniard is on a F1 circuit...
as quoted in The Guardian (2005)

CHAPTER
FIVE

Unforgettable Commentary

Words and wisdom
of those behind the mic on
race day...

"

Unless I'm very much mistaken... and I am very much mistaken!

"

Murray Walker

A classic "Murrayism" from Formula One's greatest commentator

"

But here comes Sebastian Vettel! He is neck and neck with Lewis Hamilton. Vettel is alongside and ahead! Ocon is also ahead, they're four abreast.

"

David Croft

Croft captures the chaotic start to the 2018 Belgian Grand Prix perfectly...

> **"**
>
> There are seven winners of the Monaco Grand Prix on the starting line today, and four of them are Michael Schumacher.
>
> **"**

Murray Walker

Only Murray...

66

That didn't work out,
Michael. You hit the wrong
part of him, my friend. I
don't think that will cause
Villeneuve a problem.

99

Martin Brundle

*Michael Schumacher's alleged underhand tactics in
attempting to crash into a rival in order to seal the
World Championship is highlighted by Brundle's
commentary (1997)*

"

This is the opportunity that Senna was looking for, and he's going through – OUT! Oh my goodness, this is fantastic! They meet, this is what we were fearing might happen during the race, and that means to say that Prost has won the World Championship. Alain Prost, World Champion of 1989!

"

Murray Walker

Legendary F1 commentator Murray Walker describes the controversial end to the 1989 Suzuka Grand Prix as Senna clashes with Prost's car. Neither finish but Prost, with one race remaining, can no longer be overtaken by Senna in the Drivers' Championship

66

Three lights, four lights,
five laps... [pause]...
go, go, go, go!

99

Murray Walker

*Murray hilariously gets his tongue tied at the start of
the 2001 British Grand Prix*

"

He fought from second on the grid, he passed Jacques Villeneuve, he took the lead, he stayed there. And Damon Hill exits the chicane and wins the Japanese Grand Prix – and I've got to stop, because I've got a lump in my throat.

"

Murray Walker

An emotional moment for Murray as the British driver is crowned World Champion at the 1996 Japanese Grand Prix – 20 years after his father Graham's death…

66

This would have
been Senna's third
win in a row if he'd
won the two before.

99

Murray Walker

"

And look at that! And colossally, that's Mansell! That is Nigel Mansell, and the car absolutely shattered. He's fighting for control, but you can see what's happened, Mansell is out of the race. Now, this could change... it will change the World Championship!

"

Murray Walker

Murray watches the drama unfold at the 1986 Australian Grand Prix

F1 facts

The pit crew of the elite
F1 teams have the pitstop
process down to a fine art
in order to get their driver
back on the track – in
2019, the Red Bull team of
Max Verstappen's car set a
record by replacing all
4 tires in just 1.82 seconds.

"

There's nothing wrong with the car, except it's on fire.

"

Murray Walker

> 66

And a buh-ruh-rilliant race for
Michael Schumacher, who exits the
chicane for the 53rd and last time to
win the 2000 Japanese Grand Prix and
the World Championship for the third
time, to give Ferrari and Italy their
dream – and look, he knows it. He is
absolutely beside himself with joy, his
ultimate dream has been succeeded. He
can now let the emotion flood!

> 99

Murray Walker

*Murray describes the emotion as Michael Schumacher
achieves his Ferrari dream (2000)*

"

Do my eyes deceive me or is Senna's car sounding a bit rough?

"

Murray Walker

Murray – the eyes, ears and mouth of Formula One!

"

Andrea de Cesaris, the man who has won more Grands Prix than anyone else without actually winning one...

"

Murray Walker

"

Stand up wherever you are, because this is a very magical moment.
You will remember where you were the day you saw a racing driver become a five-time World Champion.

"

James Allen

Allen's memorable lines as Michael Schumacher seals victory at the 2003 French Grand Prix

❝
And now excuse
me while I interrupt
myself!
❞

Murray Walker

"

If is a very long word in Formula One. In fact, 'if' is F1 spelled backwards.

"

Murray Walker

If only it was!

66

We've got a lunatic on the track!

99

James Allen

*Allen's shock at seeing priest Neil Horan
running down the Hangar Straight in the 2003 British
GP at Silverstone – a stunt that somehow didn't
end in disaster*

66

Even in five years'
time, he will still be four
years younger than
Damon Hill.

99

Murray Walker

66

The lead car is unique,
except for the one behind
it which is identical.

99

Murray Walker

F1 facts

Silverstone launched
the first Formula
One Drivers' World
Championship
race with the
British Grand Prix
on May 13, 1950

> 66
> # And all I can say to that is bullshit.
> 99

James Hunt

During the 1989 Monaco Grand Prix, Murray Walker attempts to explain René Arnoux's claims that he was struggling to get to grips with naturally aspirated F1 cars after driving with turbo power for the majority of his career. Co-commentator Hunt responds with a line that almost leaves Murray speechless.

"

The young Ralf Schumacher has been upstaged by teenager Jenson Button, who is 20...

"

Murray Walker

Even Murray couldn't have made some of these lines up!

66

You might not think
that's cricket, and it's not,
it's motor racing.

99

Murray Walker

Interviewer: "The most exciting moment during the race weekend?"

Kimi: "I think so it's the race start, always."

Interviewer: "The most boring?"

Kimi: "Now."

"

He's got a mental age of 10! For being himself, he should receive a permanent suspension.

"

James Hunt

Hunt lets rip on driver Jean-Pierre Jabouille, who had developed a reputation for being an unhelpful back-marker. During the 1983 Australian GP, Jean-Pierre's driving was particularly bad, resulting in the former F1 champion's brutal tirade

66

That's history.
I say history because it
happened in the past.

99

Murray Walker

66

Nigel Mansell is in third
position! He's gone up
from seventh to sixth to
fourth to fifth and now
to third.

99

Murray Walker

CHAPTER
SIX

The Chequered Flag

Winning races and seeing that chequered flag – there's no feeling like it...

"

Just leave me alone, I know what to do.

"

Kimi Räikkönen

Kimi's famous line heard over the team radio after he had taken the lead in the 2012 Abu Dhabi Grand Prix – the shot was fired at his Lotus race engineer who was, in the Finn's opinion, providing too much data. Räikkönen was proved correct by winning his first race in more than three years

66

Of course, there are
moments that you wonder
how long you should be
doing it because there are
other aspects which are
not nice, of this lifestyle.
But I just love winning.

99

Ayrton Senna

"

No race has ever been won in the first corner; many have been lost there.

"

Garth Stein

American writer and producer Stein's poignant observation in his book The Art of Racing in the Rain *(2008)*

"

I'm willing to take any amount of pain to win.

"

Lewis Hamilton

> **"**
>
> It is better to go into a corner slow and come out fast, than to go in fast and come out dead.
>
> **"**
>
> **Stirling Moss**

"

Winning is definitely
the ultimate goal,
the lessons learned
when I don't win
only strengthen me.

"

Lewis Hamilton

66

I retired simply because I didn't
have the passion and motivation
anymore; I was tired.
At the time I thought, 'Well,
I had a great time, there is the end.'
At some moment, there is the
right time to call it an end.

99

Michael Schumacher

*The German superstar on accepting it was time
to quit F1 (2006)*

66

We have to remember these days. There is no guarantee they will last forever. Enjoy them as long as they last.

99

Sebastian Vettel

Vettel's words over the team radio at the 2013 United States Grand Prix having secured his fourth drivers' championship – prophetically, it was also his last

"

As a driver, you've always got
to believe in your heart that
you've got what it takes to win
it. You've always got to believe
in yourself. You've always got to
arrive on the day and believe it
can happen. You've always got to
believe in the positives.

"

Lewis Hamilton

"
You commit yourself
to such a level where there
is no compromise.
You give everything you
have, everything,
absolutely everything.

"

Ayrton Senna

"

I was never 'Mad Max'.
I was just Max who was
trying to get the best
result for the team. As a
driver I will always be the
same guy.

"

Max Verstappen

*The Dutch star – a road warrior in style only, not name
– as quoted on GPFans.com (2019)*

"

I always say that my ideal is to get pole with the minimum effort, and to win the race at the slowest speed possible.

"

Alain Prost

Happy to trundle over the finish line in first! As quoted in Autosport (1993)

"

And suddenly I realized that I was no longer driving the car consciously. I was driving it by a kind of instinct, only I was in a different dimension.

"

Ayrton Senna

Many believed him to have been on another plain when he drove...

66

Time is of the essence and I don't have much essence left.

99

Graham Hill

*The very essence of the Formula One champion
of 1962 and 1968!*

"

Each driver has its limit. My limit is a little bit further than others.

,,

Ayrton Senna

66

You will never know the feeling of a driver when winning a race. The helmet hides feelings that cannot be understood.

99

Ayrton Senna

"

Tell you the truth,
I hate Monaco. It's like
riding a bicycle
around your living room.

"

Nelson Piquet

*The controversial Brazilian gives an insight into why
he never won a Grand Prix in Monaco – as quoted in the
New York Times (2008)*

❝

I look at myself as
someone who has been
very lucky – my job is also
what I enjoy most in the
world, and I can make my
life doing it.

❞

Fernando Alonso

"

Forget everything and just drive.

"

Lando Norris

66

First, you have to finish.

99

Michael Schumacher

66

My dad once said that you meet a much nicer class of person there, but I'm not sure.

99

Damon Hill

Damon – son of F1 great Graham Hill – didn't entirely agree with his father's thinking about starting from the back of the grid! (1993)

66

I think you improve on
everything; you're never
perfect.

99

Max Verstappen

66

Being second is to be the first of the ones who lose.

99

Ayrton Senna

A glimpse into a winner's mentality...

66

It's not a bad feeling
at all, is it?

99

Ayrton Senna

*Senna celebrates his second F1 World Championship
in 1990 after crashing with Prost and gaining revenge
for the 1989 battle between the two rivals*

66

If you no longer go for a gap that exists, you're no longer a racing driver.

99

Ayrton Senna

The Brazilian legend tells commentator Jackie Stewart why he took risks – which some considered unsportsmanlike – in the 1990 Japanese Grand Prix